SPACE HOPPERS

UNDEAD ON URANUS

TOMMY DONBAVAND

NASEN House, 4/5 Amber Business Village, Amber Close, Amington, Tamworth, Staffordshire, B77 4RP

Rising Stars UK Ltd.
7 Hatchers Mews, Bermondsey Street, London SE1 3GS
www.risingstars-uk.com

Text © Tommy Donbavand 2014
Design and layout © Rising Stars UK Ltd. 2014
The right of Tommy Donbavand to be identified as the author of this work has been asserted by him in accordance with the Copyright, Design and Patents Act, 1998.

Published 2014

Author: Tommy Donbavand
Cover design: Sarah Garbett @ Sg Creative Services
Illustrations: Alan Brown for Advocate Art
Text design and typesetting: Sarah Garbett @ Sg Creative Services
Publisher: Fiona Lazenby
Editorial consultants: Jane Friswell and Dee Reid
Editorial: Fiona Tomlinson and Sarah Chappelow

All rights reserved. No part of this publication may be reproduced, stored in a retrieval system or transmitted in any form by any means, electronic, mechanical, photocopying, recording or otherwise without the prior permission of Rising Stars.

British Library Cataloguing in Publication Data.
A CIP record of this book is available from the British Library.

ISBN: 978-1-78339-324-4

Printed in the UK by Ashford Colour Press Ltd, Gosport, Hampshire

CONTENTS

Meet the Space Hoppers	4
COSMIC Training Session	6
Chapter 1: Flopsy	10
Chapter 2: Dead Scary	18
Chapter 3: Surrounded	28
Chapter 4: Bite Back	33
Glossary	46
Quiz questions	47
About the author	48
Quiz answers	48

MEET THE SPACE HOPPERS

Name: Dan Fireball
Rank: Captain
Age: 12
Home planet: Earth
Most likely to: hide behind the Captain's chair and ask timidly, "Are we there yet?"

Name: Astra Moon
Rank: Second Officer
Age: 11
Home planet: The Moon
Most likely to: face up to The Geezer, strike a karate pose and say, "Bring it on!"

HS INFINITY

Name: Volt
Rank: Agent
Age: Really old!
Home planet: Venus
Most likely to: puff steam from his shoulder exhausts and announce, "Hop completed!"

Name: Gus Buster
Rank: Head of COSMIC
Age: 15
Home planet: Earth
Most likely to: suddenly appear on the view screen and yell, "Fireball, where are you?"

COSMIC 🪐 TRAINING SESSION
HISTORY OF THE SOLAR SYSTEM

VOLT

> Greetings new recruits!
>
> My name is Volt and I shall be your cyber-teacher for today.
>
> You should read this section because if you wish to become COSMIC 🪐 agents you must know the history of the Solar System.

Long ago, adults used to be in charge of everything. They had jobs, ran governments and were in charge of television remote controls.

Children were forced to stay in school until the age of 18. They had to do everything their parents told them. They were only given small amounts of currency, known as 'pocket money'.

There were lots of problems. Adults polluted the Earth and then went on to do the same — or even worse — on the remaining eight planets of our Solar System. In fact, for a long time, adults even refused to call Pluto a real planet!

So, in the year 2281, the children took over.

Adults were made to retire at the age of 18 and were sent to retirement homes on satellites in space. Children just needed three years at school, so most children were working by the time they were eight years old.

The Solar System quickly became a much happier, safer and cleaner place to live.

However, not all of the adults liked having to retire at the age of 18. Some of them rebelled and escaped from their retirement homes on satellites in space. 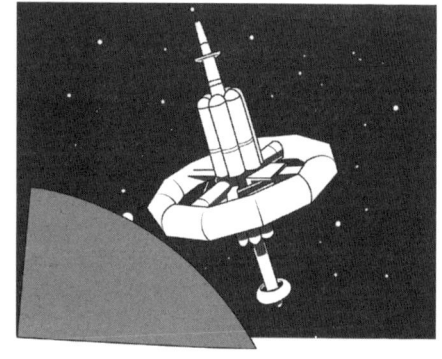 They began to cause trouble and commit crimes.

That's why COSMIC was created:

Crimes
    Of
        Serious
            Magnitude
                Investigation
                    Company

The worst of these villains was known as The Geezer. The purpose of COSMIC was to stop The Geezer from committing crimes.

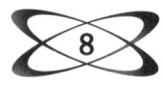

Members of COSMIC flew around the Solar System solving mysteries and bringing badly behaved adults to justice. The COSMIC spaceships could navigate an invisible series of magnetic tunnels called the Hop Field, so they were called Space Hoppers.

I myself, was a member of one such team of Space Hoppers, alongside the famous agents - Dan Fireball and Astra Moon.

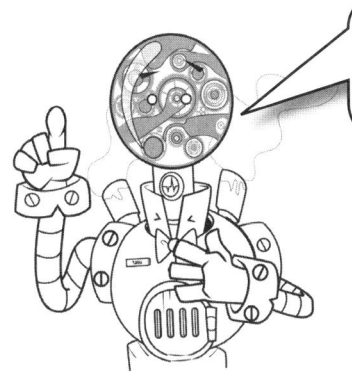

If you turn the page, you can read about one of the scariest missions we ever undertook …

CHAPTER 1

FLOPSY

HS INFINITY DATA LOG
MISSION REPORT 3:
UNDEAD ON URANUS
REPORT BEGINS ...

The doors to the command deck of the HS Infinity whooshed open. Second Officer Astra Moon stepped in carrying a small box wrapped in silver paper.

"The post droid has just been," she said, dropping the box on to the Captain's desk.

"Shhh!" said Dan Fireball from his captain's chair. "Can't you see I'm reading?"

Astra raised her eyebrows. "Reading?" she smiled. "A real book? With words?"

Dan looked up. "Of course it's a real book!" he said. "What else would it be?"

"I thought the only books you ever took out of the COSMIC library were ones that you had to colour in!" joked Astra.

"Ha ha, very funny!" sneered Dan. "Actually, I'll have you know that this is a very interesting natural history book."

"Really?" said Astra. "What's it called?"

Dan checked the title on the cover. *"Caring For Your Pet Bunny Rabbit."*

"You're getting a pet rabbit?" said Astra in surprise.

"I've already got one," said Dan. "Well, at least — I did have. He died."

"Oh, I'm sorry to hear that," said Astra. "Losing a pet can be tough."

"It was," agreed Dan with a sigh. "Flopsy was such a wonderful bunny. He had long ears, soft white fur and a little pink nose that twitched when he was eating a carrot."

"It sounds like you miss him a lot," said Astra. "When did he die?"

"Last night," said Dan, snapping his book closed. "My parents have posted me the body so that I can bury it."

Astra edged back from the package on the desk. "You mean — your little Flopsy is in there?" she croaked. "Dead?"

Dan examined the package. "Just as well he is dead. My dad forgot to put any air holes in the box."

Astra clamped a hand over her mouth as the doors to the command deck hissed open again and a brass robot entered, balanced on a single wheel. Clouds of steam pumped from exhaust pipes built in to his shoulders.

"I'm sorry to interrupt, Master Dan, but there is an urgent message coming in from COSMIC HQ."

Dan leapt into his captain's chair. "Put it on screen please Volt."

Volt tapped a command into his computer keyboard and a large, serious face filled the view screen at the front of the ship.

"Chief!" said Dan, with a salute. "What's up?"

"We've got a problem with Uranus." said Chief Gus Buster.

"Uranus?" repeated Astra. "But, that's always been the most peaceful planet in the Solar System!"

"Indeed, Miss Astra," said Volt. "The atmosphere there is one of great calm — that's why many people choose it to be their final resting place."

"You mean where dead people are buried?" asked Dan.

Volt nodded.

Dan's eyes grew watery. "Dead!" he said. "Like my little Flopsy ..."

"Uranus is a gas giant," Volt added. "So there is an interesting smell to the air — although that doesn't affect the dead people's noses, for obvious reasons."

"Noses?" sniffed Dan. "My little Flopsy had a twitchy, pink nose ..."

Astra ignored him. "What's the problem, Chief?" she asked the figure on the screen.

"It appears that the dead on Uranus have found a new lease of life!" said the Chief. "They've been climbing out of their graves since dawn."

Astra's eyes grew wide. "You mean they're zombies?"

The Chief nodded. "As crazy as that seems, yes."

"So I need you three down on Uranus as soon as possible," said the Chief. "We're on borrowed time here."

Dan wiped the tears from his eyes. "Did you say *burrowed*?" he asked.

"No, Captain Fireball — I said *borrowed*! Now get to Uranus!" The screen hissed, then went blank.

"Sounds like a tricky mission," said Astra, typing co-ordinates for the Hop Field into the computer. "Prepare to Hop!" Then she slammed her palm down on a large, yellow button sticking up from her desk.

And that's when Dan finally burst into tears. "Flopsy used to hop!" he wailed, as the HS Infinity leapt sideways into one of the invisible magnetic tunnels that make up the Hop Field, connecting every planet and moon in the Solar System.

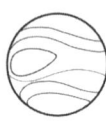

DEAD SCARY

The ship landed near the entrance to one of the largest cemeteries on Uranus. Dan and Astra fixed their helmets to the collars of their COSMIC spacesuits, then pressed the button to activate the air lock.

Dan was just about to open the exterior door when Astra noticed he had the silver-papered parcel from home tucked under his arm.

"Where are you going with that?" she asked.

"Well," said Dan. "Volt told us that lots of people choose to be buried here on Uranus, because it's so peaceful ..."

"That's right," said Astra.

"Then, what better resting place for my beloved pet rabbit?" said Dan.

"There are special burial grounds for pets here, Miss Astra," Volt explained as he rolled up to join them.

"Alright," said Astra. "But we deal with the zombies first and sort Flopsy out later, do you hear me?"

Dan started blinking back tears again. "Flopsy used to hear things," he sighed. "With her long ears ..."

"And you can stop all that nonsense, as well!" Astra snapped. "You have to pull yourself together. There's no telling what could be on the other side of that door."

"You're right," said Dan, striking a brave pose. "Captain Fireball — ready for action!"

He opened the exterior door. There was something waiting for them on the other side. Or, rather, someone. A stocky boy of around 15 years of age, dressed in a smart black suit and wearing a space helmet.

"Chief!" cried Dan and Astra together.

The Chief saluted. "Dan, Astra, Volt …"

"What are you doing here?" Astra asked.

"It was my great grandfather's funeral today," Chief Gus Buster explained. "I've been here since early morning."

"So, you've seen these zombies crawling out of their graves yourself?" said Dan.

The Chief nodded. "It's not a pleasant sight — especially now they've started to bite people. Anyone who gets bitten becomes infected with the zombie virus and starts acting like one of the walking dead themselves."

"That's terrible!" exclaimed Astra.

"I agree," said the Chief. "So, I need to know you're ready for whatever this mission throws at you. What equipment are you carrying?"

Astra checked her utility belt. "Portable computer, stun spray, first aid kit and back-up batteries for my communications wristband."

"Good," said The Chief. He turned to Dan. "And you?"

Dan showed his parcel. "Dead rabbit in a box, sir."

The Chief blinked, not saying anything for a moment. Then Volt wheeled up to him.

"I shall be carrying the Captain's equipment today, sir," said the robot.

"Okay," said the Chief. "Now, the last sighting of the zombies was—"

"No need to tell us, Chief," Astra interrupted. "Zombies at twelve o'clock ..."

Dan checked his watch. "Good," he said. "That gives us an hour."

"No, I mean they're right behind you!" said Astra. "And heading this way!"

Dan and the Chief spun round to discover a mob of about a hundred corpses shuffling in their direction.

The zombies were in all states of decomposition. Some looked as though they'd just woken up from a long nap, while others were falling apart, leaving a trail of detached arms and legs in their wake.

Among the group were visitors to the cemetery and mourners at the day's funerals who had been bitten by the original zombies.

They all had green skin and they were all chanting: "Brains! Brains!"

"What do we do?" asked Astra, nervously.

"The scientists back at COSMIC HQ are trying to find a way to stop them," replied the Chief. "Until they get back to me with a solution, all we can do is keep living people out of their way."

"Starting with us!" cried Dan. "Come on!"

The group leapt down from the ship's platform and ran across the green grass of the cemetery, away from the approaching zombies. They ducked between the gravestones and dodged clouds of thick, purple gas.

"It is this gas that gives Uranus its peculiar smell," said Volt. "If you and Miss Astra were to remove your helmets …"

"The stench would get us before the zombies did!" Astra butted in. "Keep your helmet on, Dan."

Dan, however, couldn't reply. "Can't we … rest … for a while …" he gasped through heavy breaths.

The Chief nodded. "We've got enough of a head start," he said. "And it looks as though most of the visitors and mourners have already been evacuated from this area. We'll rest here for a few minutes before carrying on."

Dan gave an exhausted salute, then he balanced his parcel on the top of the nearest gravestone and sank down on to the grass.

Chief Gus Buster carefully lifted up the box from the gravestone and peered at it. "What is this thing?' he said.

And that's when a rotting rabbit's paw burst up through the silver wrapping paper. The paw was quickly followed by a head ... a head with blazing red eyes and sharp, gnashing teeth.

"Flopsy!" exclaimed Dan, leaping to his feet. "You've come back to me!"

Just then, Flopsy sank his teeth deep into Chief Gus Buster's arm.

"Oh dear," said Dan.

SURROUNDED

Dan, Astra and Volt jumped back in alarm as Flopsy dropped to the ground and began to shuffle between them, snapping and growling. Green froth bubbled from the rabbit's mouth, and his ears flicked back and forth angrily.

"I don't think Flopsy's very well!" cried Dan.

"Of course not!" said Astra. "It's a zombie rabbit! Whatever made all those people come back to life has done the same to your pesky pet!"

Dan squealed as Flopsy sprang at him. "What do we do?"

"I have an idea, if you don't mind, Master Dan," said Volt.

"Anything!" yelled Dan.

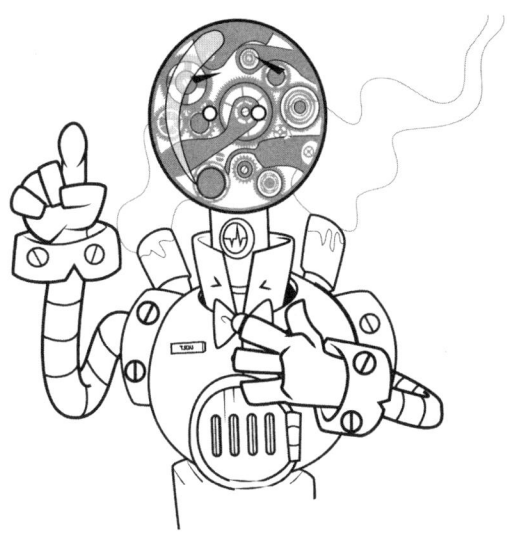

With a burst of steam, Volt darted forwards. He reached down and grabbed the zombie rabbit by the ears then, with a flick of his robotic wrist, he hurled the zombie pet as far away from the group as possible.

Dan watched as Flopsy flew away, landing in a patch of distant bushes. "You threw my rabbit away!" he shouted at Volt.

"You did tell me I could do anything," Volt reminded him.

"I didn't mean turn him into a boomerang!" cried Dan.

"If I may be so bold," began Volt, "Flopsy is most definitely not a boomerang. Boomerangs come back."

"Quiet, both of you!" snapped Astra, hurrying over to the Chief. He was crouched on the ground, his head bowed and his wrist clutched in his other hand.

"Are you okay, Chief?" she asked.

Chief Gus Buster snapped his head up to stare at Astra with burning red eyes. His skin had turned pale green, and he was frothing at the mouth.

"Brains!" groaned the Chief. "Brains!"

"Oh no!" said Astra, backing away. "Flopsy's bite has infected him. The Chief is a zombie!"

"I believe this may be a good time to return to the ship," advised Volt.

"Too late for that!" said Dan, pointing.

The other zombies — the ones they'd originally been running away from — had appeared from among the nearby gravestones. They shuffled towards them, arms outstretched.

"Brains! Brains!"

Dan and Astra spun round. Zombies were now approaching from all sides. They were surrounded.

"Volt!" cried Astra. "Is there anything you can do?"

"I'm afraid not, Miss Astra," said the robot. "I doubt that my soft brass exterior will stand up to an attack by angry teeth. I'm in as much danger as you are."

"Do we have anything we can use as a weapon?" Dan asked.

"Only my stun spray," replied Astra.

"Then what are you waiting for?" demanded Dan.

Astra unclipped a small bottle from her utility belt. "Just trying to choose which one of the zombies I've got time to use this on!"

Suddenly, the Chief hurried towards them, snapping his teeth. "Brains!"

Astra sprayed him in the face with her stun gun. The Chief stopped for a second, licked his lips, then continued his attack.

BITE BACK

Suddenly, someone yelled "WAIT!", and everything stopped. The advancing zombies froze in mid-attack.

Dan and Astra looked up at the undead surrounding them. It was as though they were standing at the centre of a circle of statues.

"Who did that?" asked Dan.

"I did!" said a figure, pushing through the crowd of corpses. It was an adult, wearing a grey cardigan and comfy slippers. The Space Hopper team recognised him immediately.

"The Geezer!" barked Astra. "The most wanted criminal in the Solar System!"

"Now, now!" said The Geezer, wagging a finger at her. "There's no need for that kind of attitude. I did just save you from becoming one of the undead, after all …"

"You froze them?" said Dan.

"Indeed!" grinned The Geezer, producing a device that looked like a TV remote control with a dial at the top.

"I have control of their body clocks, and I just paused them all."

"Body clocks!" said Astra. "So that's how you're doing this."

"Very clever of you to work it out so quickly!" said The Geezer, impressed.

"Hang on," said Dan. "How's he doing what? What have you worked out quickly?"

The Geezer sighed. "Shall I tell him, or shall you?

"I'll go first," said Astra. She turned to Dan. "Every living creature has a body clock," she explained. "It starts as soon as they're born. It tells them when to grow, age and — eventually — die."

"Is that why I can hear ticking when I'm in bed at night?" asked Dan.

"No, sir," said Volt. "That is your alarm clock."

The Geezer stepped forward. "All I had to do was find a way to gain control over the body clocks of the people buried here, and then put them back a few years with the help of this nifty little gadget."

Dan's eyes grew wide. "So, their bodies would think they should still be alive, and woke them up from being dead!" he exclaimed.

"Exactly!" cried The Geezer. "Now, I have an army of undead to do my will!"

"What happened to your old age pensioner henchmen?" said Dan.

The Geezer rolled his eyes. "They demanded a holiday!" he sighed. "But zombies have no need for holidays. With my army of corpses, I shall conquer every planet in the Solar System!"

"Not if we stop you!" snarled Astra.

"No chance of that, I'm afraid!" said The Geezer. "You see, I'm just about to restart the body clocks of this lot. You'll be zombie food in a matter of seconds."

"NO!" yelled Dan as The Geezer's finger hovered over the handheld gadget. "No one's biting me! Quite the opposite in fact ..."

He leapt forward and sank his teeth into the back of The Geezer's hand. The old man cried out in pain and dropped his device. It fell on to a gravestone and shattered into a dozen pieces.

Slowly, as though struggling to wake up, the zombies around them began to stir.

"You fool!" roared The Geezer, rubbing at the back of his hand. "You've broken my gadget! Now I have no control over them!"

"Then you'd better do the same as us and run!" exclaimed Astra. "Now!" She grabbed Dan and Volt by the wrist and pulled them out of the circle of corpses. They ran as the zombies stretched out their arms towards them.

The Geezer screamed and ran in the opposite direction — towards Shady Acres, his spaceship retirement home, parked on a far away hill.

"He's getting away!" moaned Dan.

"And so are we!" Astra reminded him. "We'll blast off and then send a message to COSMIC telling them that Uranus is a no-go area." She glanced back at the zombies, who were now giving chase once more.

"What about the mission, Miss Astra?" asked Volt.

"We can't win them all," said Astra. "We've bitten off more than we can chew here."

Dan stopped running. "That's it!" he said.

"What's it?" said Astra.

"Biting!" said Dan, smiling.

"Which is exactly what that lot behind us will do if we hang around here!" snapped Astra. "Come on!"

"No," said Dan. "I think I can fix this. If a zombie bites a human they turn into a zombie, right?"

"That is correct, sir," said Volt.

"But what if a human bites a zombie …?" asked Dan.

Astra's eyes widened in alarm. "Okay," she said. "You've officially lost your mind!"

"Possibly," said Dan. "But it's also possible that I've found a way to put an end to all this." Then, before Astra or Volt could stop him, he set off running back towards the crowd of hungry zombies.

Astra and Volt looked at each other, then hurried after him.

"Chief!" cried Dan, skidding to a halt beside his brain-hungry boss. "This might hurt a little…" Then Dan leaned in and bit the older boy hard on the ear.

"Brains!" roared the Chief angrily. "Brai …! What did you do that for?" He rubbed at the bite mark on his ear.

Dan grinned. It had worked! The Chief's eyes were brown again, and the green tint to his skin had already disappeared. "I'm nipping this mission in the bud!" grinned Dan. "Now, get biting!"

Astra and Volt arrived to help as Dan and the Chief turned left and right, biting arms, chomping down on fingers and chewing necks. Volt did his best to hold the remaining zombies at bay while the three humans tucked in. It was tough going, but, one by one, the zombies transformed back into humans.

An hour later Dan, Astra and the Chief sat on the ramp of the HS Infinity, rubbing their aching jaws. Standing around the ship were hundreds of normal people, none of whom wanted to crack anyone's head open and feast on the goo inside.

The door to the ship hissed open and Volt wheeled out. "I have repaired the device, Miss Astra," he said, handing over The Geezer's handheld gadget. "You now have complete control over the body clocks of everyone on Uranus."

"Thanks," said Astra, taking the gadget. "Okay, everyone gather round ..."

The crowd fell silent.

"I'm about to reset your body clocks," Astra announced. "For some of you, that means you'll be heading back to your graves. That's the way it has to be, I'm afraid."

"Don't you worry about it, young lady!" cried a female voice from the back of the crowd. "Coming back to life is far too much like hard work, if you ask me!"

There were cries of "Yes!", "Too right!" and "Hated it!" from the group.

Astra hit the reset button on the computer. Those who had risen from their graves wished the visitors farewell, then shuffled back to continue with their eternal rest.

"Job done!" said the Chief.

"I just wish The Geezer hadn't got away," groaned Dan.

"The Geezer may have got away," said Astra with a smile, "but this little fella didn't."

Volt opened a hatch in his side and produced a tiny, white baby rabbit.

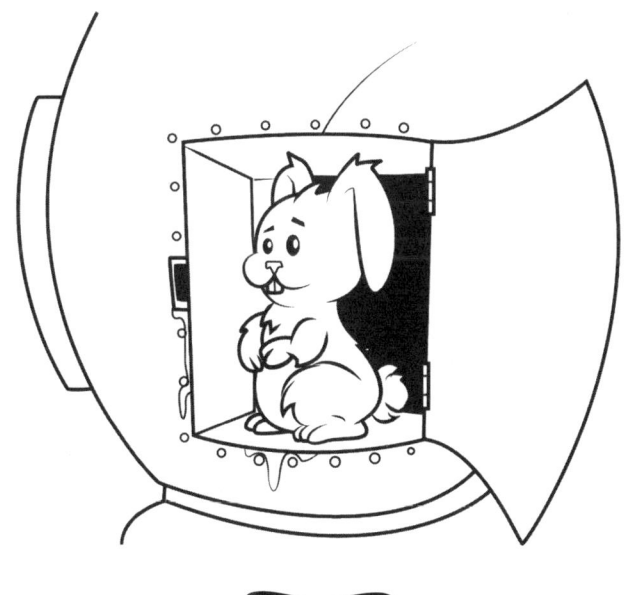

"Flopsy!" exclaimed Dan, taking the bunny and cradling him in his arms. "But, how?"

"There's one body clock I reset back to the start," said Astra. "Now you can have him as a pet all over again."

Dan smiled widely. "Thank you—oo—oo … AH-CHOO!" He sneezed and wiped his nose on the back of his hand. "Oh dear!"

"What's the matter?" asked the Chief.

"I'm allergic to rabbits!" sniffed Dan. "AH-CHOO! Always have been. That's why I left him at home with my mum and dad. AH-CHOO!"

"I don't believe it ..." muttered Astra.

"Here," said Dan, handing the baby bunny back to Volt. "Send him home to my parents, will you? And put some air holes in the box this time!"

"AH-AH-AH-CHOO!"

THE END

Now read *Nursery on Neptune* to find out what The Geezer gets up to next!

GLOSSARY

allergic — being sensitive to something, e.g. food or pollen, and having a reaction to it

body clock — the body's built-in way of knowing how to behave at different times of day

currency — the kind of money used in a country

decomposition — being broken down or rotting

device — a machine or tool used for a particular task

eternal — lasting forever

evacuated — removed from somewhere thought to be unsafe

mourner — close friend or relative of someone who has died

stench — a very strong, unpleasant smell

transformed — changed shape or appearance

utility belt — belt for carrying a range of tools and equipment

QUIZ QUESTIONS

1. What type of planet is Uranus?
2. Who meets the Space Hoppers on Uranus?
3. What do the zombies do to living people?
4. What has happened to Flopsy?
5. What effect does the stun spray have on zombies?
6. Who is controlling the zombies?
7. How is he controlling the zombies?
8. What does The Geezer plan to do with his army of corpses?
9. How do the Space Hoppers restore the zombies back to being normal people?
10. Why does Flopsy have to go back to live with Dan's mother and father?

ABOUT THE AUTHOR

Tommy Donbavand writes full-time and lives in Lancashire with his family. He is also the author of the 13-book *Scream Street* series (currently in production for TV) and has written numerous books for children and young adults.

For Tommy, the best thing about being an author is getting to spend his days making up adventures for his readers. He also writes for 'The Bash Street Kids' in *The Beano*, which excites him beyond belief!

Find out more about Tommy and his other books at www.tommydonbavand.com

QUIZ ANSWERS

1. A gas giant
2. The Chief
3. Bite them and infect them with the zombie virus.
4. It has become a zombie-rabbit.
5. It has no effect on them and does not stop their attack.
6. The Geezer
7. He has control of their body clocks with a handheld gadget.
8. Conquer every planet in the Solar System.
9. By biting them.
10. Because Dan is allergic to rabbits.